THE MOTHMAN AFFIRMATIONS

THE MOTHMAN AFFIRMATIONS

DICTATED BY
MOTHMAN

TRANSCRIBED BY
MIKE DIGRAZIA

THE MOTHMAN AFFIRMATIONS

Cover Design by Mike DiGrazia
Print book interior design by Mike DiGrazia

ISBN: 9798996170128

FOR
SAS
JERSEY
AND
CHUPA

SPECIFICALLY NOT FOR
SKUNKAPE
(I FIND HIM UNCOUTH AND OFFENSIVE)

A Word from Your Author

Greetings, humans.

It is I... Mothman. Yes, *that* Mothman.
Red eyes, wingspan of unsettling proportions,
spotted near and around bridges
shortly before "incidents."

You may have seen me in blurry photographs,
niche documentaries, or on that one guy's
conspiracy podcast your cousin listens to.

I get it. I've got a reputation.
"Harbinger of doom." "Omen of disaster."
"Giant winged aberration ruining date nights
since 1967."

But let me set the record straight:
I'm not here to cause catastrophes.

I'm here to warn you.

I'm like a smoke alarm with wings.
A sentient, anxiety-riddled forewarning
with better than average night vision.

Somewhere along the way, I realized something:

You humans aren't just afraid of the future.
You're afraid of *yourselves.*

So, I decided to write this book.
Because maybe what the world needs right now
isn't just another forecast of doom...

Maybe what it needs is a few words of wisdom from
someone who knows a thing or two about
deep introspection, and being misunderstood.

For 100 Days You Will Receive:

An Affirmation,
because even nocturnal omens
deserve a little positive self-talk.

A Reflection,
to help you think deep thoughts
in dark places.

And a Ritual,
because life is better with
a little self-imposed structure.

This book is not a substitute for therapy.

It is, however, the emotional equivalent of being firmly picked up by a magnificent eight-foot winged enigma and gently placed on the right path.

Possibly at midnight.

Possibly during a thunderstorm.

So, flap your proverbial wings, sharpen your instincts, and let's start this journey together.

We'll navigate the fog. We'll haunt our insecurities. We might even fix some internal bridges before they collapse.

And remember:

You're not too weird.
You're just the right amount.

I will be watching. I'm *always* watching.

Your emotional support beastie,

MOTHMAN

A Word from Your Co-Author

Hello, friends!

You may be wondering how it came to be that the one and only MOTHMAN chose *me* to help bring his book of affirmations to the world.

Well, let me tell you the tale.

Some time back I took a trip to Sedona, AZ to see what all that Vortex hubbub was about.

While taking an early evening hike around Bell Rock, a butte known for its distinctive bell shape and its status as a powerful energy vortex, I encountered what at first I thought was a giant gray bird perched atop a rock formation a little further up the trail from where I had stopped to catch my breath. I eyed it quizzically as I slurped some water from my camel pack.

As I continued on and grew closer, it became alarmingly clear just how big this *bird* actually was.

I stopped about 15 feet away and stared at it. It rotated its head toward me like a statue coming to life. I gulped! Its eyes were like shiny red baseballs and it felt as if they were peering straight through my soul.

Chills ran up my spine as the thing laggardly stood from its gargoyle-like squat and extended to its full height, which appeared to be 7 or 8 feet tall as far as I could figure.

I would later learn that he was actually standing on his toes, which is something he does when trying to make himself look more intimidating. They are ridiculously long for no good reason and, honestly, kinda gross. Sorry, pal.

It outstretched what revealed itself to be a lanky, humanoid arm and pointed its spindly finger directly at me. My heart skipped a beat.

I turned to run, but mid-step, the unmistakable rattle of the one Nope Rope you don't want to encounter while hiking through the Arizona desert, stopped me dead in my tracks.

I peered down and there it was, not a foot and a half in front of me… the biggest rattlesnake I'd ever seen!

I glanced over my shoulder to see the giant *thing* still pointing at me and then back to the rattler, who was now swirling himself into a coil.

I took a slow step backward towards the thing and, astonishingly, *it spoke.*

"I wouldn't do that if I were you. That's a rattlesnake", it said in a shockingly Transatlantic accent.

All I could do was blink. "Wh-what?"

It continued pointing. "That right there," it said again, calmly. "That's a rattlesnake. Very dangerous."

I shot a glance to the coiling monster
and back to the thing.

"I KNOW," I yelped, starting to take another step back. "What do I do?"

"Definitely not that", it sighed as two massive wings unfurled from its back and it leapt from its perch.

A hiss brought my attention back to the snake just in time to see it launching itself toward me.

Time froze and my life flashed before my eyes.
All the shouldas, wouldas and couldas.
Every last one of them flicked through my noggin
like a greatest hits sizzle reel on crack.
I was a goner. I knew it.
I made peace with the universe and closed my eyes…

Then, suddenly,
the thing I would soon come to know as *Mothman*,
plucked me into the air and straight outta danger!

The rattler landed with a hollow thump as we soared into the sky above and I let out a triumphant laugh. Mothman laughed as well. We *laughed together* as we circled the area looking for a safe, scenic spot to land.

Long story short, Mothman saved my life that day.

And we bonded.

It turned out we had a lot more in common
than one would imagine:

Among other things, we both have an affinity for the strange and unusual, we both share a love of black coffee, we both have a similar sense of humor and we both really love Godzilla films.

His fave is Mothra VS. Godzilla.
Obvi!

I could go on and on,
but maybe the most important is this:
we both understand what it's like
to feel a bit out of step with the world.
And we both believe that's where the magic lives.

So when he came to me with his idea for this book, I agreed to do the legwork to get it off the ground.

I mean, clearly, someone with a lurking schedule as extensive as Mothman's does not have the time to allocate to something as tedious as designing and publishing a book.

Oh, I should also say that
although I support Mothman's overall message,
I don't necessarily agree with
EVERYTHING he says within these pages.

We're pals and all, but he's still Mothman,
and he can be a little *out there* sometimes.

Now, go forth and soak up some wisdom, friends.

Sometimes you find it
in the most unlikely of places.

Peace and all that jazz!

Mike DiGrazia

1-5

Day 1

I am the calm preceding the storm,
as well as the storm that follows.

You are not either/or —
you're the full atmospheric event.
You bring intensity and relief,
chaos and tranquility,
protein bars and cheeseburgers.
Embrace your full spectrum.

Make yourself a snack that feels ritualistic.
Arrange it like an offering.
Consume it with intention and gratitude.

MOTHMAN

Day 2

I am an imperfect masterpiece.

Perfection is a flat line. Your growth curves like a spiral staircase. Keep ascending.

Find an unfinished piece of art,
writing, or effort of some sort.
Gaze upon it fondly.
Thank it for existing,
in spite of it not being "finished."

Day 3

I hold multitudes,
and some of them are truly bizarre.

You are a haunted house of delights.
Some rooms have water slides.
Some rooms speak in tongues.
All are open for business.

Introduce yourself today with a secret title.
("Hi, I'm Bob — Eater of Worlds.")

MOTHMAN

Day 4

The universe doesn't need me to be impressive.
It just wants me to be authentic.

Stars don't hustle. They just burn.
Flowers don't innovate. They just grow.
You're doing just fine.

Be astonishingly average
at something today.
Do it with joy.

Day 5

I am on the verge of something quietly magnificent.

You may not see the shift yet,
but tectonic plates move slowly
before mountains rise.
Stay malleable.

Write a message to your future self.
End it with:
"I already believe in you."

list 3 humans that you love

6-10

Day 6

I am the master of my own twilight.

Between light and dark lies your sacred space — a place to dream, doubt, and dance.

At dusk, stand outside
and watch shadows stretch.
Whisper a secret only the night
(and perhaps, me, should I be lurking)
can keep.

Day 7

I will wear my battle scars like constellations.

Each experience is a star in your personal
cosmos, guiding you through storms
and quiet nights alike.

Trace a scar or imperfection
with your finger.
Imagine it glowing softly,
like a cosmic beacon.

Day 8

I embrace the beautiful oddity of my existence.

There is no normal here.
You are a beautiful riddle
wrapped in luminous wings.

Wear two mismatched shoes today
on purpose.
Revel in the chaos.

MOTHMAN

Day 9

***I am not a problem to solve
but a mystery to cherish.***

The universe delights in puzzles
that never fully unfold.
Your complexity is a divine gift, not a flaw.

Write a poem about one thing
people misunderstand about you.

MOTHMAN

Day 10

I will not negotiate with my inner saboteur today.

That voice telling you that you're
not worthy? Its name is Self-Doubt
and it's a real jerk.
You *are* worthy.
And deep down you know it.

Give your self-doubt an adequate name
(e.g., "Doc McDoucheins").
Politely dismiss it from all meetings today.

MOTHMAN

list 3 foods that you love

11-15

Day 11

I carry the wildness of
deep midnight skies in my heart.

In darkness, stars are brightest.
Your soul shines brightest when you
embrace the wildness within you.

Look at the night sky (or a dark ceiling).
Make a wish that no one else
will ever know.

Day 12

I am a bridge between worlds — seen and unseen.

Your presence connects the ordinary and the extraordinary.
You are magic walking among mortals.

Carry a small object (a feather, stone, or acorn) as a talisman for your liminal power.

Day 13

I will nurture the soft places inside me.

Tenderness is strength
disguised in cashmere.
Care for your inner self
as if it were a magical garden.

Write a gentle letter to yourself,
praising the parts you usually hide.
Like your unusually long toes.

Day 14

I honor the strange paths that led me here.

Every odd turn, every missed step,
every detour was part of your
sacred unfolding.

Map your journey —
literal or metaphorical —
with doodles, notes,
or a messy scribble
in the journal of you.

MOTHMAN

Day 15

I am endlessly becoming —
forever an idiosyncratic mystery.

There is no end, only metamorphosis.
Celebrate the eternal flight
of your soul's wings.

Light a candle or lantern.
Watch the flame flicker
and vow to keep shining,
no matter how dark the night.

list 3 places you love to lurk

16-20

Day 16

I am not obligated to explain my wingspan.

People will always ask what you are,
where you came from, what your "deal" is.
Let them.
Not everything needs an origin story.
Some beauty is meant to be bewildering.
You don't owe anyone a backstory.
Only a moment of real presence.

Find a piece of clothing, an accessory,
or a look that makes you feel
a little strange and a lot powerful.
Wear it without apology.
Bonus points if it flutters when you move.

Day 17

I belong in this world,
even when I don't feel like I fit.

Even puzzle pieces that don't fit the picture
still have shape, weight and beauty.
Perhaps you are from a different box.

Find a mirror. Look into it.
Say:
"You're real. You're here. That's enough."
Then do a couple squats
and maybe some wing stretches.

Day 18

I am allowed to pause without guilt.

Even galaxies take breaks
between explosions.
You're a living, breathing organism,
not a productivity app.

Take a 3-minute break today
where you do nothing but breathe
and stare dramatically out a window.
Bonus if it's raining.

Day 19

I carry ancient wisdom
in my bizarre little bones.

Your body is a time capsule.
Every ache, every scar, every stretch
is a message from an ancestor
who also stubbed their toe.

Trace your hand on a piece of paper.
Label each finger with
a strange but noble trait
("Left pinky: stoic under pressure.")

MOTHMAN

Day 20

I am an inter-dimensional delight.

You think you're just one person?
Human, please.
Other versions of you are out there
break dancing in zero gravity.
They believe in you.

Leave yourself a note somewhere hidden.
Sign it from "Alternate You."
Make it outlandishly encouraging.

MOTHMAN

list 3 smells that you love

21-25

Day 21

I don't have to explain my transformation to anyone.

The inter-dimensional caterpillar
never files a progress report.
The moth(man) emerges
without a press release.

Choose one thing about yourself to quietly upgrade today. Say nothing. Just glow.

Day 22

Even my detours are destinations.

Wandering is sacred.
Confusion is holy.
Sometimes the side quest is the quest.

Take a different route today
(physically or emotionally).
Look for a sign (literal or cosmic).
Pretend it was left just for you.
Perhaps it was.

MOTHMAN

Day 23

I am a creature of pattern and paradox.

You may spiral, but look closely —
those spirals are fractals.
They repeat with style.
Chaos is just sophistication in disguise.

Draw a spiral on your hand.
Let it remind you:
every return is also a new beginning.

Day 24

I do not need permission to begin again.

There is no cosmic timekeeper.
Reboot when you need to.

Choose something today to reboot:
your mood, your to-do list, your name.
(Temporarily become "Spark Nightshade."
You earned it.)

MOTHMAN

Day 25

I am a sacred disruption in the timeline.

Your existence shifts probabilities.
You are a beautiful fluctuation that makes the simulation more interesting.

Do something small but unexpected today.
Write your grocery list on your hand.
Wear two different shoes.
Confuse the grid.

list 3 things that you adore

26-30

Day 26

I am not behind.
I'm on my own calendar,
currently in the month of Rebirthuary.

Linear time is a suggestion, not a rule.
You bloom when your own
internal season says so.

Create a calendar event called
"Expand Weirdly."
Set an alert.
Celebrate with an unreasonable
amount of coffee and lurking.

MOTHMAN

Day 27

***I can do hard things —
especially while complaining, grunting
and covered in cookie crumbs.***

Grace isn't the absence of mess.
It's the courage to move forward with
marinara dripping down your white t-shirt.

Pick one mildly heroic task.
Do it today.
Reward yourself with
a ceremonial piece of rotting fruit
or some yummy plant sap.

Day 28

I radiate mysterious
main-character energy.

Someone out there is telling stories
about you with awe.
Even when you're just at home
microwaving an egg in a coffee mug
because the frying pan is still dirty from
when you made tacos last Tuesday.

Enter every room today
as if you have a bad ass soundtrack.
Choose your theme song.
Hum it with authority.

MOTHMAN

Day 29

I am more than what I produce.
I am also what I daydream.

Productivity is not identity.
Your idle thoughts are architecture
for unseen worlds.
Napping is spiritual labor.

Stare at a ceiling for five minutes
and breathe.
No agenda.
No guilt.
Just you, your breath and the ceiling.

MOTHMAN

Day 30

I have boundaries.
Even the most mysterious fog has edges.

Being soft doesn't mean being shapeless.
Even a moth avoids flames it doesn't trust.
You can be luminous and still say "no."

Say "no" to one thing today.
Out loud.
Even if it's to a candy wrapper.
Make it sound final.

place your finger on the dot

breathe... you are here

31-35

Day 31

I am a beautifully unreliable narrator of my own story — and that's okay.

Memory is performance art.
Your past is a collaborative hallucination
between neurons and nostalgia.
Own the edits.
All of them.

Retell a memory today with dramatic flair.
Add fog. Add suspense.
Bonus if you give your childhood dog
a set of magnificent wings
and glowy red eyes.

MOTHMAN

Day 32

I can hold grief and giggles at the same time.

Sorrow and absurdity often travel together,
like zebras and ostriches.
Feel both. Laugh-cry. Cry-laugh.
It's all sacred.

Watch a video of a cat kneading a dog.
Then light a candle for someone you miss.
Feel your chest expand
like wings in flight.

MOTHMAN

Day 33

I am not confusing.
I am complicated.

You're not a malfunctioning machine.
You're a mysteriously unique ecosystem.
Some people may think
they need a manual,
but they just need to listen more deeply.

Choose one secret today.
Whisper it into a jar.
Put the lid on.
Label it "Cosmic Truth."
Place it somewhere important.

MOTHMAN

Day 34

I have survived every strange day so far.
I am a collector of odd triumphs.

Your trophy case may only be filled with metaphorical gold and emotional sunlight, but it's real. And it's yours.

Write down three "wins" from your life
that no one has ever celebrated.
Pump your fists and shout "Triomphe!"
after reciting each one.
Let the walls know your truth.

MOTHMAN

Day 35

I am allowed to not know what's going on.

Clarity is overrated.
Some days, life is like blurry security cam footage from a gas station in Point Pleasant.
That's okay.
You're still on the tape.

Write down three things
that you don't understand.
Fold them into paper airplanes
and release them into the wild.

MOTHMAN

list 3 things you no longer need

36-40

Day 36

I may not be everyone's cup of coffee,
but I am someone's
chocolate covered espresso bean.

Not being understood
is a sign of originality.
Some people need instructions.
Others just need vibes.
Be the vibes.

Send a nonsensical compliment
to someone you trust.
Example:
"You have the unmitigated strength
of a 12-toed Megayeti."

MOTHMAN

Day 37

I do not chase closure —
I summon clarity on my own terms.

Closure is a myth sold by Hallmark
and a mediocre song by Taylor Swift.
Real healing doesn't always end cleanly.
That's fine. You're still evolving.

Write down a name, situation,
or lingering ache.
Burn it (safely), bury it,
or stick it in the freezer.
Whisper:
"This chapter ends when I say it ends."

Day 38

I am not late.
I am arriving precisely when I am needed.

Punctuality is a mortal concept.
Real timing, is cosmic intuition.

Miss something small today.
Then dramatically reappear with
donuts and no explanation.
(Preferably jelly-filled or Maple Longjohns)

MOTHMAN

Day 39

I am allowed to evolve out loud.

Transformation isn't always tidy.
Wings sprout peculiarly.
Pupae ooze. Let your molting be visible.
It may inspire someone else.

Wear something today that makes you feel
like a new version of yourself.
Extra points for big red sunglasses
and a fuzzy gray sweater.

MOTHMAN

Day 40

I trust my instincts —
even when they arrive festooned in anxiety.

Sometimes your gut feelings wear
strange costumes to get your attention.
Don't ignore them
just because they're awkward.

Have a dialogue with your anxiety.
Write it a letter.
Start with:
"Hello. I see you and I know what you are."

MOTHMAN

finish the sentence

one of the things
i like about myself is

____

41-45

Day 41

Today I will flirt with the void,
but not give it my digits.

Staring into nothing can be healthy.
Just remember,
you don't owe the abyss anything.
Ghost it if it gets needy.

Stare dramatically
out a window for 3 minutes.
Whisper something cryptic like
"By the gods... it's happening."
Then resume normal tasks.

MOTHMAN

Day 42

I accept myself —
even the versions that
are still under construction.

You're not a finished product.
You're a prototype tested in live conditions.
That makes you unique
in all your iterations.

Write yourself a permission slip
for one thing you haven't "earned" yet.
Carry it in your pocket.
Use it with reckless abandon.

MOTHMAN

Day 43

I am allowed to rest —
even if I haven't "earned" it.

Rest is not a reward. It's a right.
Planets don't hustle. They just rotate.
You're allowed to nap like cosmic royalty.

Lie down somewhere inappropriate
(but safe). The floor. Porch.
A pile of pizza boxes.
Say:
"This is my throne now."
Rest for at least 7 minutes. Maybe 8.

Day 44

I do not have to monetize my joy.

It's okay to do weird little things
just because they feel good.
Not everything is a brand.
Some things are just sacred nonsense.

Do something joyfully pointless today.
Sing into a plastic cup.
Paint a rock and toss it somewhere random.
Dance with no camera on.
Let capitalism tremble.

Day 45

Even when I glitch, I glow.

You're not a malfunction.
You're just catching transmissions from
beyond the polite dimension.
Beep-boop-beep-bzzzz with pride.

Fake a computer error today.
Freeze mid-sentence. Blink.
Say "Rebooting..."
and carry on like nothing happened.
Observe reactions.

draw a self-portrait

46-50

I
LIKE
ME

Day 46

I do not chase validation.
I wait patiently for it in the dark.

There's a certain power in stillness.
You don't have to broadcast your brilliance
or hustle for attention.
You simply exist, wings folded,
eyes glowing faintly in the treetops —
and eventually, they look up.

Today, do something quietly excellent.
Don't post about it. Don't explain it.
Let it hum in the background of your myth.
That's where legends grow.

Day 47

I let go of what I was told I should fear.

That locked room
in your Grandmother's basement.
People who are different.
The Mothman of Point Pleasant.
You were warned about them all —
but what if the thing you fear
is actually the fear itself?

Write a list of five things you fear.
Circle the one that feels the most ludicrous.
Compliment it aloud.
"Thank you for making me cautious.
Now be gone with you!"

MOTHMAN

Day 48

*Today I commune with the chaos gently,
like a dragonfly atop the snout of a crocodile.*

Sometimes life is trash strewn
on the side of the road.
Sometimes it's a magnificent ripple
in a peaceful pond.
You're allowed to be both.

Pick up one chaotic thing you've been
avoiding (that pile of papers,
that pile of nail clippings).
Gently acknowledge it.
Then offer it a gummy bear.
Yes, really.

Day 49

I am not a problem to fix.
I am a landscape to explore.

You are not a spreadsheet of issues.
You are strange and glorious terrain —
— crags, waterfalls, quicksand and all.

Draw a map of your internal world.
No accuracy required.
Just landmarks like
"Cave of Smelling My Fingers
When No One is Watching"
and "Valley of Replaying Interactions I Had
with Someone Yesterday Over and Over
and Over Again."

MOTHMAN

Day 50

My past selves cheer me on
from liminal space bleachers.

You've survived every version
of yourself so far.
They didn't disappear —
they just joined the spectral fan section
of your soul stadium.

Write a note from a past self
to your current one.
Maybe the teenage you.
Or version of you from last month
who was so into lurking
that they forgot to eat lunch or dinner.

list 3 things you think are beautiful

51-55

Day 51

I do not perform my healing.
I live it, unevenly and sincerely.

You don't owe anyone a linear recovery arc.
Healing is chaotic and can often involve
eating whole pizzas
under a weighted blanket.

Write a permission slip to yourself:
I may heal messily.
Sign it. Stamp it. Eat a bagel.
You're doing amazing.

MOTHMAN

Day 52

I am a myth in the making.

Legends aren't born polished.
They start as strange stories whispered
by people who saw someone or something
glowing a little too brightly in the middle of
the night in a gas station parking lot.

Write the first line of your own myth.
Example:
"There was a luminous being
who danced insouciantly in the darkness
with the grace of a gazelle..."
Frame it and hang it somewhere ridiculous.

MOTHMAN

Day 53

I don't need to make sense to be sublime.

Great art, Mothmen,
and unscheduled freakouts
all have one thing in common: mystery.
Coherence is optional.
Presence is everything.

Wear a color that doesn't "go"
with the others.
Tell someone a dream you had,
even if it ends with
"...and then the toilet exploded and
launched me straight into planetary orbit."

MOTHMAN

Day 54

I can say "no" without having to write a full on thesis about it.

Boundaries don't need footnotes.
"No" is a full sentence, a protective ward,
and an energetic fist-bump
from your higher self.

Practice saying "no" aloud five times
with different dramatic inflections.
Bonus points for incorporating echo effects
or fog machines.

MOTHMAN

Day 55

I am not lost.
I am just loitering creatively.

Some days you won't know where you're going. That's fine. Mothman spends most of his time wandering near abandoned power stations and it's working for him.
You're not off-track —
you're on a detour of destiny.

Take an unnecessary walk.
Follow any raven that makes eye contact.
When you return, write down three ominous but motivational phrases.
Example:
"The dread-soaked clouds loom large.
As do you."

MOTHMAN

list 3 reasons mothman is the best

56-60

Day 56

I thrive in the misunderstood margins of reality.

You may or may not have been
built for center stage —
but you thrive in back alleys of thought,
forgotten dream corridors,
and moments that reek of déjà vu.

Take a walk with no destination.
Let intuition lead.
Stop when something feels significant,
even if it's just a flickering light
or weirdly placed chair.

MOTHMAN

Day 57

Even in entropy,
I shine strategically.

Chaos doesn't mean failure —
it's just the dance floor of becoming.
You're not falling apart;
you're innovating on the molecular level.

Do something joyful and pointless
while surrounded by disorder.
Sing in a cluttered room.
Dance barefoot among dirty laundry.
Just be... defiantly.

MOTHMAN

Day 58

I accept compliments like sacred offerings, not suspicious packages.

Deflecting praise is so last century. Try absorbing it into your radiant psychic membrane and whispering "yes, I know" to your third eye.

The next compliment you receive, simply say "thank you" and then mentally bow like a majestically Gothic beastie receiving a gift of rotting fruit.

MOTHMAN

Day 59

I am allowed to recalibrate without warning.

You're not a vending machine.
You don't owe consistent output
at the push of a button.
Some days are just for static and rebooting.

Cancel one minor obligation today.
Replace it with lying on the floor
and staring at the ceiling
while softly humming
your personal reboot tone.

Day 60

When I vanish,
my presence leaves echoes.

Sometimes disappearing for a minute is survival. You don't have to be visible to be impactful. Mothman sightings last seconds — the stories last lifetimes. Don't be afraid to pull back. Let your silence speak volumes.

Take one hour today to vanish from all communication.
No pings, no screens, no updates.
Sit in the stillness of your own presence.

place a booger in the circle

i dare you

61-65

Day 61

I choose alignment over achievement.

The world shouts: "Do more!"
But your soul whispers: "Be real."
Alignment is quiet, soft,
and sometimes looks like
not giving a single glowing poop.

Take one task off your list today.
Replace it with something wildly aligned.
Like gazing at the stars.
Or spending time with your friend
Mothman, because, even though you say
you're out of town, you forgot that you
didn't turn the tracking off on your phone
and he knows you're at sitting at home
avoiding him.

MOTHMAN

Day 62

***I carry the wisdom of haunted libraries
and forgotten playlists.***

You've gathered strange knowledge over
lifetimes — some of it from
late-night YouTube rabbit holes,
some of it from dreams where
your teeth began to fall out
while taking a test you forgot to study for
and simultaneously realizing
that you weren't wearing any clothes.

Create a "personal lore" playlist.
Include songs that feel like
liminal elevators or cryptic glances
from strangers. Listen while holding a mug
of coffee in both hands as if it were sacred.

MOTHMAN

Day 63

I do not fear transformation —
I molt with unabashed flair.

Growth isn't linear.
It's a series of weird molts
where you leave pieces of yourself
in metaphysical rest stops.
It's itchy. Sometimes uncomfortable.
But necessary.

Write down one belief you've outgrown.
Crumple it and throw it over your shoulder.
Say,
"May my next form be even more
preternatural."

MOTHMAN

Day 64

My intuition is not broken;
it's just speaking in riddles again.

Gut feelings don't always speak fluently. Sometimes they mutter in Morse code or communicate through synchronized avian behavior rituals.

Observe your surroundings for three small omens today. Interpret them as if the universe is awkwardly trying to flirt with you. Respond in kind.

Day 65

I do not chase closure —
I collect open loops like peculiar stones.

Life rarely ties its shoelaces.
Unanswered questions
and unresolved conversations
are invitations to stay curious.

Write down one unresolved
thing in your life.
Instead of solving it,
frame it like artwork.

MOTHMAN

finish the sentence

i am pretty darn cool
because

____

66-70

Day 66

I reserve the right to be an enigma
wrapped in a hoodie(or lavish wings)
wrapped in night fog.

You owe no one complete clarity.
Ambiguity is not avoidance — it's texture.
Let your mystery breathe.

Spend today resisting
the urge to over-explain.
When someone asks,
"What do you mean?"
smile slowly and say,
"Exactly."

MOTHMAN

Day 67

I find meaning in the absurd and comfort in the bizarre.

Why should enlightenment
only come from yoga retreats?
Sometimes it lives in parking lot seagulls
or singing into a fan.

Engage in a delightfully useless act today.
Make a bridge out of toothpicks.
Compliment a table.
Let nonsense be nectar.

Day 68

I respect my past selves — even the overly dramatic ones.

You've worn many skins — some shiny,
some tear-stained, some covered in dust.
They were all trying their best.

Write a short letter to
a former version of yourself.
Thank them. Forgive them.
Assure them that you've got it from here.

Day 69

***I am a liminal being
thriving in transitional times.***

You are not lost —
you're just between chapters.
Doorways, dusk, and awkward silences
are where you do your best work.

Stand in a literal doorway today.
Linger. Breathe.
Say,
"Here, in the in-between, I bloom."
Then vanish mysteriously,
or go make some coffee.

MOTHMAN

Day 70

My glow is not for everyone —
and that makes it sacred.

If some people wear shades
around your radiance and call you
"too much", that's fine.
Not all creatures are built to
appreciate brilliance.

Choose one weird trait of yours
and praise it out loud like it
just won an award.
Bonus points for giving a thumbs up
to your own reflection.

MOTHMAN

list your 3 favorite non-humans

MOTHMAN

71-75

Day 71

I am not over-the-top.
I am a limited-edition mythic occurrence.

You are not excessive. You are rare.
Some people just don't have the bandwidth
to receive your full signal.
That's their problem.

Write a dramatic myth about yourself.
Begin with "Long long ago,
in the time before algorithms..."
and end with
"...and that's how they made the world
just a little bit brighter."

MOTHMAN

Day 72

I embrace the glory in minor chaos.

A crooked painting.
An unwashed cereal spoon.
A single sock that manifests
without its other.
These are holy.
Control is brittle.
Chaos is compost for the soul.

Let one small thing today
go gloriously wrong without correcting it.
Observe. Breathe.
Nod sagely,
like an ancient deity
watching time unravel.

MOTHMAN

Day 73

Even my detours are part of the divine blueprint.

You weren't "off track" — you were gathering crucial vibes in the swamp. Trust the long, strange route you linger on. It knows things.

Find something you once thought was a mistake. Thank it out loud. Bonus points for bowing reverently to the chaos of your past.

MOTHMAN

Day 74

I am fluent in silence
and dialects of awkwardness.

You don't need to be eloquent.
Your presence is poetry.
Even your pauses are concertos
in the orchestral void.

Spend ten minutes today
not responding right away.
Let pauses bloom.
Imagine a subtitle under you reading:
"Processing inter-dimensional cosmic data,
please wait..."

MOTHMAN

Day 75

I am magnetized to the peculiar and repelled by the predictable.

There's no shame in being
allergic to normalcy.
Your compass points toward the strange,
and that's a superpower —
not a malfunction.

Wear something today
that subtly unnerves at least one stranger.
A hockey mask.
A set of official Mothman-branded wings.
Socks over your shoes.
Claim it's for
"cosmic realignment purposes."

MOTHMAN

draw a heart and put your name in it

76-80

Day 76

I am not behind.
I am on my own timeline,
which occasionally runs parallel
to sandhill crane migration season.

Comparison is for the birds.
No one else has your map.
Your pacing is perfect —
even if you occasionally nap
in metaphysical attics.

Draw a timeline of your life,
and be sure to make it squiggly, looping,
and full of symbols.
Add a star where you're currently standing.
Whisper,
"Right on track, you fierce wonder!"

MOTHMAN

Day 77

I am not confused —
I'm just temporarily multidimensional.

Clarity is overrated.
You're unfolding.
Sometimes that means existing in
twelve moods simultaneously
while slurping a cup of coffee
and questioning multidimensionality.

Choose a feeling that's been lingering.
Assign it a fictional species and habitat.
Honor it.
Name it something exotic like
"Anxietosaurus Wrecks."

MOTHMAN

Day 78

My transformation is not linear.
It's an ever-winding staircase.

You may revisit the same emotions,
but you meet them
from new heights each time.
Just because they look familiar
doesn't mean you haven't grown.

Draw a spiral.
Write a word on each loop that describes
how you've changed over the last five years.
Frame it and hang it over your toilet.
Or better yet,
someone else's toilet.

MOTHMAN

Day 79

I can embrace uncertainty
without screaming — most of the time.

You don't need to know what's next to be okay. You are a lighthouse in a fog made of smooth jazz. Just flash your light and hum.

Fold a paper fortune teller. Write all the things you might become inside of it and pick one. Read it aloud in a detective voice. That is now your temporary destiny.

MOTHMAN

Day 80

I do not chase closure.
I haunt open endings with style.

Not every chapter gets a clean conclusion.
That's fine.
You're here to linger, sparkle,
and maybe leave a cryptic Post-it note
on the way out the door.

Find something unfinished
(a letter, a drawing, a bowl of cereal).
Add one final flourish.
Declare it deliberately incomplete.
Walk away like you've dropped the mic.

MOTHMAN

list 3 of your favorite songs

81-85

Day 81

I am my ancestors' most absurd and glorious dream.

They never imagined you would wear
slip-on shoes and eat sushi while
contemplating quantum sadness.
But here you are. Existing beautifully.

Do one small thing today
that your great-great-grandparent
couldn't even have imagined:
Send a meme into space.
Take a ride in a driver-less vehicle.
Look up what
Homoheterocerus occidentavirginianus
means on your high-powered
computer telephone.

MOTHMAN

Day 82

*I am soft, strong
and slightly radioactive.*

Contradictions are part of the charm.
You can be gentle and unapproachable,
glowing and grounded.
Embrace your inner paradox.

Make a list of 3 things
that feel incompatible about you.
Celebrate each one with a small offering
(e.g., a compliment, an bag of Jelly Babies,
a pat on your back).

MOTHMAN

Day 83

My uniqueness is not a bug in my system.
It's my programming.

You didn't arrive here by accident.
You're the result of careful cosmic mischief.
Your quirks are the user interface
of your soul.

Write a user manual for yourself.
Include
"Operating Instructions,"
"Caution Warnings,"
and a list of songs
that unlock your godmode.

MOTHMAN

Day 84

The night does not frighten me.
We have an understanding.

The dark isn't always dangerous.
Sometimes, it's just where ideas germinate
and the cosmos hums.
Stillness is sacred.

Turn out the lights for five minutes.
No phone. No distractions.
Just breathe and listen
to what the darkness is trying to tell you.
If it's something about
a guy named Indrid Cold,
politely disregard.

MOTHMAN

Day 85

***When I disappear, it's not retreat.
It's transformation.***

Cocooning is not quitting.
Sometimes you go dark so you can
reemerge with better wings
and bigger, glowyer eyes.

Log out. Sign off.
Power down early tonight.
Wrap yourself in a blanket and imagine
the static reorganizing your soul.
Wake up enigmatic AF!

MOTHMAN

list 3 of your favorite colors

86-90

Day 86

I am the unskippable cutscene
in someone's spiritual journey.

You're a formative encounter.
A strange phrase.
A glowy-eyed detour.
Don't underestimate the impact
of your strange little orbit.

Today, say something cryptic
but kind to a stranger.
Then walk away
as if you've fulfilled a prophecy.
Bonus if you wear a cape
or cape-adjacent item.

MOTHMAN

Day 87

I am the kind of mystery that improves over time.

People won't always get you on the first try.
That's a feature, not a flaw.
Great novels confuse in chapter one.

Write a 3-line summary
of your current emotional state
as if it were the back cover
of a Fortean novel.
Read it in your best dramatic voice.
Frame it if it slaps.

MOTHMAN

Day 88

I am not lagging behind.
I am marinating.

Progress isn't linear, and neither are you.
You are becoming seasoned, tender,
and terrifyingly enigmatic
in exactly the right timeline.

Today, do one thing slowly.
Alarmingly slowly.
Eat. Walk. Dress. Lurk.
Let the universe adapt to your pacing.

MOTHMAN

Day 89

Even in my crumpled state,
I am a work of art.

You don't have to be polished
to be precious.
You are a collage of stumbles, spray paint,
receipts, and emotional pocket change.
A walking installation piece.

Take one item you were going to throw
away and turn it into something
odd and beautiful. Tape a bottle to a sock.
Name your trash sculpture "Mike."

MOTHMAN

Day 90

My energy is odd and powerful.
Like an abandoned satellite
still transmitting love.

You don't have to be in orbit to matter.
Your signal reaches further than you think.

Send a message (text, letter, carrier moth)
to someone you haven't spoken to in ages.
No explanation.
Just a signal:
"Still here. Still flying."

MOTHMAN

list 3 things that bring you joy

91-95

Day 91

I am not lost.
I am exploring aggressively.

Being direction-less isn't failure —
it's freedom with panache.

Take a walk with no destination.
Follow a weird noise, a strange smell,
or a passing squirrel that looks like
it knows something.
Bonus points if you freak yourself out.

Day 92

I am a limited edition haunting.

You're not supposed to be understood
by everyone. You are a custom frequency.
A velvet disturbance.
The reason someone will one day say,
"I swear I felt something."

Leave a cryptic note for your future self.
Hide it in a coat pocket,
a shoe, or beneath a planter.
Forget it completely.
Let your future be delightfully confused.

MOTHMAN

Day 93

My wings are not freaky —
they're extravagant!

Body image is hard when people
only photograph you in mid-swoop.
But you're not here to be understood;
you're here to unsettle and inspire.
Own your weirdness.
Be the best majestic sky-goblin you can be.

Stretch your arms wide
and flap three times (do it).
Make an unidentifiable screeching sound.
Bonus points if you startle a pet
or a human who shares your domicile.
The spirit of Mothman moves through you.

MOTHMAN

Day 94

I may not have been built for this world.
But I upgraded it by showing up.

You're not here to fit in.
You're here to tilt the axis just enough
that reality hiccups.
Your difference isn't an error —
it's an upgrade.

Stand somewhere slightly inconvenient
today. A stairwell. A grocery aisle.
The wrong side of a revolving door.
Long enough to be noticed,
but not long enough to be removed.
Remind the world it has edges.

MOTHMAN

Day 95

I haunt gently. I love fiercely.
I leave footprints in dreams.

You may never know how deeply
you've touched someone's life.
That word you whispered.
That awkward kindness.
That time you stood nearby
like a guardian angel.
Don't underestimate the gravity
of small hauntings.

Leave a message today for someone without expecting anything back. A note. A meme. A compliment on their uncanny energy. You never know which gentle echo becomes someone's salvation.

MOTHMAN

List 3 things you are grateful for

96-100

Day 96

My intuition may not come with receipts — but it rarely lies.

You don't always need logic.
Sometimes you just know.
You feel the change in the air
and the tension in your wingtips.
Trust that.
You're tuned to frequencies others pick up
— and that's a gift.

Make one decision today based purely on
gut feeling. Doesn't have to be big —
just intentional.
A turn you take, a snack you eat,
a cryptic text you send.
Bonus points if it feels mildly prophetic.

MOTHMAN

Day 97

I am allowed to shed versions of myself like old exoskeletons.

The Mothman you read about in 1967
is not the Mothman writing this book.
Evolution is messy. You molt,
you change shape, you outgrow things
with dramatic flair. Embrace it.
Past You served a purpose.
Present You is wiser.

Write down a version of yourself
that you've outgrown.
A habit, a profession, a fear.
Rip it up and scatter the pieces
somewhere symbolic.
(Don't litter. Compost, maybe.)

MOTHMAN

Day 98

I do not chase signs. I am the sign.

You've spent enough time waiting for
omens, symbols, synchronicities.
You are the harbinger now. You are the
shimmering glitch in someone else's
pattern. You're what they write about
in their journal under
"weird but meaningful."

Wear or carry something today
that makes you feel like an omen.
A ring. A feather. A stare.
Stand in someone's peripheral vision
just long enough to make them question
everything. Then smile warmly.
You're the message.

MOTHMAN

Day 99

I contain the chaos of
a thousand missed phone calls —
and the peace of never answering.

You are not obligated to respond instantly.
You are not a blinking notification light.
Rest is your divine right.
Silence is not absence —
it's sacred bandwidth.

Turn off one notification source today.
Let it rest. Let you rest.
If the world needs you, it knows where to
find the cursed payphone in the woods.

MOTHMAN

Day 100

I don't overthink.
I conduct full internal séances.

Your mind doesn't wander —
it hosts conferences.
Yes, you may occasionally spiral into
speculative dread about a text you sent six
years ago. But that's not a flaw. That's depth.
You commune regularly
with thought-ghosts.

Write down the spiraling thought
burdening you today. Fold it once.
Whisper, "You are free to haunt someone
else now." Then place it in your
sock drawer. Let the ghosts nap for once.

MOTHMAN

reflections

ABOUT
MOUTHMAN

Mothman is a self-proclaimed renaissance man.

He's a philosopher, a sculptor, a painter, a Lepidopterist, a gas station coffee sommelier and a professional lurker.

He loves freaking people out, staring into the void, giving questionable advice and pulling "silly pranks" that history often records as "acts of God."

He is currently transient and prefers to go wherever the winds take him.

He holds a degree in Lurking from The School of Hard Knocks.

ABOUT
MIKE DIGRAZIA

Mike DiGrazia paints things, makes noises,
occasionally writes coherent sentences,
and is mildly eccentric.
He currently resides on Earth and finds it tolerable.

CHECK OUT MIKE'S OTHER STUFF

FINE ART AND BOOKS
instagram.com/digraziart
www.digraziart.com

MOVIE ARTWORK
instagram.com/digmovieart

POZITIVYTRON PROJECT
instagram.com/pozitivytron
www.pozitivytron.com

www.ingramcontent.com/pod-product-compliance
Lightning Source LLC
LaVergne TN
LVHW022042200926
848481LV00003B/755
* 9 7 9 8 9 9 6 1 7 0 1 2 8 *